M000018790

pocket posh® sewing tips

Jodie Davis
and
Jayne Davis

Andrews McMeel
Publishing, LLC

Kansas City • Sydney • London

POCKET POSH® SEWING TIPS

copyright © 2012 by Jodie Davis and Jayne Davis. All rights
reserved. Printed in China. No part of this book may be used or
reproduced in any manner whatsoever without written permission
except in the case of reprints in the context of reviews.

Andrews McMeel Publishing, LLC
an Andrews McMeel Universal company
1130 Walnut Street, Kansas City, Missouri 64106

www.andrewsmcmeel.com

12 13 14 15 16 SHZ 10 9 8 7 6 5 4 3 2 1

ISBN: 978-1-4494-0982-1

Library of Congress Control Number: 2011932655

Cover illustration © 2010 jill bliss/jillbliss.com
Hand drawings © 2012 lia Owens-Williamson

ATTENTION: SCHOOLS AND BUSINESSES
Andrews McMeel books are available at quantity discounts with
bulk purchase for educational, business, or sales promotional use.
For information, please e-mail the Andrews McMeel Publishing
Special Sales Department:
specialsales@amuniversal.com

contents

acknowledgments

Stitching makes me sew happy!

—Anonymous

Sewing has always been a part of our lives. In fact, we feel a bit sorry for those who say, "Oh, I can't even sew on a button." We jump right in and show them how. We thank everyone who has ever held a needle in her hand. We thank family and friends and teachers who have encouraged us and inspired us and helped us hone our skills through the years. We thank both known and unknown forebears who passed along this sewing gene, a "let's try this" attitude, and love of cloth. And we especially give thanks for having this wonderful stepdaughter–stepmother thing.

why sew?

why sew?

> When I'm a grown-up woman
> With hair up on my head
> I'll sit and sew the whole night through
> And never go to bed
>
> —*Anonymous*

Sewing is back in vogue, and it's more popular than ever. More than sixty-four million Americans are sewing at last count, dividing projects equally between clothing and home decor.

We sew for many reasons. Sewing is a creative outlet. It's satisfying to finish a project and say, "I made that!" We sew to have clothing that fits and is comfortable to wear. We sew to have clothing that is unique and ours alone, not one of tens of thousands cranked out overseas. We sew because fabric is beautiful and we love the tactile feel of it. We sew to give to others and sometimes to save money. We sew for the sheer joy of it.

Whether you're sewing on a button or stitching a ball gown, you'll find tips in this book that will make the task faster and easier. They will help make you a fearless sewer, ready to take on any project, big or small.

the basic sewing kit

the basic sewing kit

Any day spent sewing is a good day.
—*Anonymous*

every household used to have a wicker sewing basket. Today we still need a place to gather all our supplies in one place. The "basket" (Fig. 1) can be as simple as an empty cigar box (D) or a more elaborate padded and compartmented basket (A) available at your local sewing store. A small plastic cabinet with drawers (B) available at home-improvement and hardware stores will keep your supplies visible. An all-purpose plastic carryall (C) available at craft stores works well, as does a tackle box.

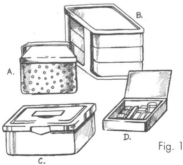

Fig. 1

basic sewing supplies for most machine- and hand-sewing projects are shown in Fig. 2 (page 6).

A. Measuring tape: Make sure it's made of a nonstretch material.

B. Small sewing scissors: Used for clipping notches, trimming, and clipping threads.

C. Large fabric shears: Used for cutting fabric.

D. Seam ripper: Clip unwanted stitches with this gadget.

E. Thimble: Saves your fingers from pricks, and is used to push the needle in hand sewing.

F. Tailor's chalk: Used to mark fabric.

G. Needle threader: Makes an easy job of threading hand-sewing needles.

H. Hand-sewing needles: It's useful to have an assortment of sizes on hand.

I. Thread: Keep a supply of basic colors—white, black, navy, beige, gray, and red.

J. Pincushion with straight and safety pins: Keep additional pins in a small container.

K. Sewing machine needles: Keep several sizes on hand.

L. Beeswax: Used to strengthen thread for hand sewing.

M. Point turner: Used to push out sewn corners when a project is turned right side out.

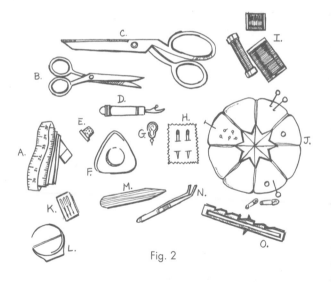

Fig. 2

N. Tweezers: Used to pick out threads after using a seam ripper.

O. Seam gauge: This is a short ruler with an adjustable flange used to measure hems and seams.

....

as times goes by you'll discover all sorts of gadgets that can simplify sewing projects. Before you know it you'll accumulate quite a few.

....

remember grandma's button tin? Well, you still need to keep a few buttons on hand. Most ready-to-wear comes with an extra button attached. Clip those and put them in your button box. Clip buttons from discarded clothing that has no future life. These will come in handy to replace shirt buttons and waistband buttons that go missing. Start out with a small plastic container you can slip in your sewing box. You'll be surprised how soon you'll move up to a larger container.

....

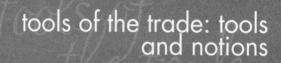

tools of the trade: tools
and notions

tools and notions

I love sewing and have plenty of material witnesses.
—*Anonymous*

keep thread snips, not scissors, by your machine. It's quicker to pick up snips to cut thread than to put your fingers through the handle holes in scissors (Fig. 3).

Fig. 3

lick your finger before you put on your thimble. This will keep it in place and prevent it from slipping.

· ·

here's a great way to keep your pins from rusting, and you'll be recycling at the same time. Take one of those desiccant packs that come in many medications and put it in your pin box. You also can use the small packets that come in shoe boxes.

· ·

a bias tape maker is a handy tool for making your own bias tape (Fig. 4) rather than using store-bought. Just be sure to use firmly woven natural fabric, as these will hold the folds better. Work on your ironing board so the finished tape can be pressed as it feeds through. Bias tape makers come in a variety of sizes for making different widths of tape.

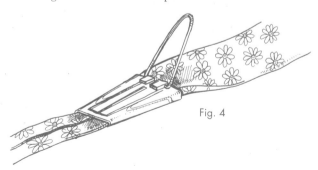

Fig. 4

the rotary cutter revolutionized quilting, and it's a useful tool for other sewing, as well (Fig 5). It makes quick work of cutting bias strips and rectangular shapes. The rotary cutter is used with a cutting mat and a grid-marked plastic ruler.

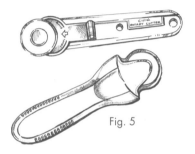

Fig. 5

blades on the rotary cutter are very sharp. For safety, be sure to close the latch on the rotary cutter every time you put it down. A few rotary cutters have blades that automatically retract when you release pressure on them after making a cut.

a safety pin makes a handy replacement for a bodkin when a cord, elastic, or ribbon needs to be threaded through a channel.

a tube turner is a wire with a latch hook at one end (Fig. 6) and is used to easily turn narrow tubes of fabric such as button loops and spaghetti straps. To use, make a small cut close to the end of a sewn tube. Slide the turner through from the opposite end and catch the cut loop with the latch hook. Pull back, easing the tube through itself.

Fig. 6

the mini iron (Fig. 7) is useful for getting into places a standard iron cannot reach. The small head allows just the needed area to be ironed and doesn't flatten the surrounding fabric. It's very handy for applying fusible trims.

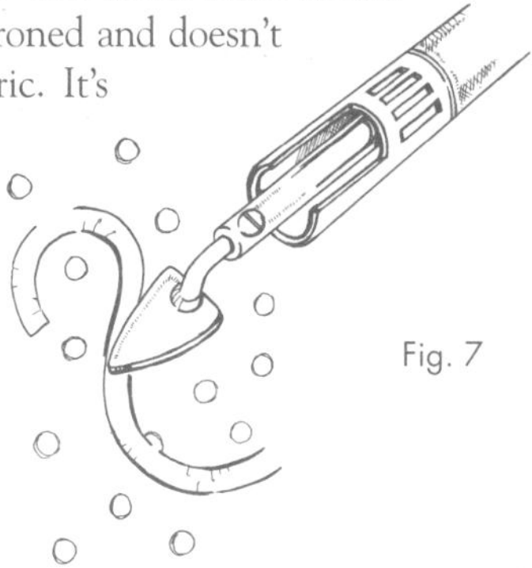

Fig. 7

13

if your iron has gunk on the soleplate, run the hot iron over a fabric softener sheet. The goo should come off on the sheet.

. . . .

another way to remove the gunk is to scrub the soleplate of the cool iron with a damp soft cloth and baking soda. Rinse out the cloth and remove any baking soda. Then, run a half tank of water through the iron to make sure the steam vents are clear.

. . . .

if the soleplate is really bad, set it facedown in a shallow baking pan or jelly roll pan. Add a quarter inch of white vinegar and leave the iron to soak a few minutes (Fig. 8). Wipe dry.

Fig. 8

14

there are many types of thread available on the market today for all types of sewing (Fig 9). Regardless of the type, always buy good-quality thread.

Fig. 9

match the thread fiber to the fabric being sewn: cotton thread for cotton or linen fabric, polyester for synthetic fabrics, silk for silk or woolen cloth.

finding the right color match sometimes can be difficult. Choose a thread that's a slightly darker shade than the fabric. A lighter shade usually will show up more. When sewing patterned fabric, use thread in the predominant color.

all-purpose thread is suitable for most sewing projects. All-purpose thread either can be cotton-wrapped polyester or 100 percent polyester. The 100 percent poly thread has a little more give, so it's often a better choice for sewing knits.

. . . .

the number on the spool of thread denotes the diameter of the thread—the higher the number, the finer the thread. A 50 weight is the best choice for most general sewing. The tension on most sewing machines has been preset at the factory for 50-weight thread.

. . . .

use the same size thread in the bobbin as in the upper threading for most general sewing.

. . . .

embroidery threads usually are 30 weight or 40 weight. Use special 60-weight bobbin thread for machine embroidery or satin stitching. This will help keep the thread from building up on the reverse side.

. . . .

if you have bobbins with one solid side you can mark the thread color with a permanent marking pen right on the bobbin. That way, you'll always have the matching bobbin even if you have three shades of navy thread.

. . . .

follow the manufacturer's directions when using notions. This especially is important for patches, gripper snaps, and grommets. The manufacturer's way is generally the very best way to use the product and obtain the most benefit.

....

want a label for your finished garment? They are very simple to produce with a computer and some inkjet paper–backed fabric sheets sold at fabric and craft stores. Use a label template and fit your design to the size template you choose. You can print thirty 2 by 1-inch labels on a letter-sized sheet. When the labels are dry, cut them out and separate them from the paper backing.

....

or check the advertising section of sewing magazines for companies that will manufacture labels for you.

....

needles

needles and how to pick the right one

needles and how to pick the right one

I cannot count my day complete
Till needle, thread, and fabric meet.
—*Anonymous*

although most sewing machine needles look alike
there are subtle differences. You'll want to have an assortment
of sizes on hand for various tasks.

. . . .

sewing machine needle thickness increases as the size
number increases. American and European manufacturers use
different numbering systems. Needles generally are marked
with both sizes, with the European size shown first.

Sewing Machine Needle Sizes

European Size	60	65	70	75	80	90	100	110	120
American Size	8	9	10	11	12	14	16	18	19

as the weight and density of the fabric increases, the needle size also should increase. And the reverse holds true: The finer the thread and the finer the fabric, the finer the needle should be. Your needle should be strong enough and have the correct point to cleanly pierce the fabric.

....

a good all-purpose size needle for most basic sewing on midweight fabrics is 80/12.

....

if the needle is too fine for the thread it can cause the thread to shred, weakening the stitch and even causing the machine to jam.

....

universal needles work on most fabrics. Ballpoint and stretch needles are specially made for knits. Sharps are used for more tightly woven fabrics. There is even a special leather needle for sewing on leather and suede and a denim needle for sewing on heavy, dense textured fabrics. A wing needle pushes fabric threads apart for heirloom stitching. In fact, there's a special needle available for almost every application.

....

using twin needles to hem stretch fabrics works like a gem and keeps the hem from rippling when sewn. It also gives a project a professional look.

. . . .

always test your stitching on a scrap of your fabric doubled using the thread and needle you'll use in the project. This way you can make any necessary changes before you get started.

. . . .

needles are cheap, so don't ruin a project by using a dull or damaged needle. Just throw it out. It's best to start each new project on your sewing machine with a new needle.

. . . .

ever put the needle in your machine backward? You find out in a hurry that something is amiss because a stitch won't form. Just remember, for almost all machines the flat side of the needle faces the back of the machine and the needle is threaded front to back.

. . . .

safely discard your used hand and machine needles. Instead of just throwing them in the trash, keep an empty prescription bottle on your sewing table and put the used needles inside it. The tops are childproof, which adds another level of safety.

---

there are four basic hand-sewing needles. In all types, the smaller the size number, the smaller the needle.

sharps: These are basic medium-length needles with round eyes and sharp points. Sizes range from 1 to 12.

betweens or quilting: These are shorter than sharps, with small, rounded eyes. These needles most often are used for hand quilting or very detailed hand sewing. Sizes range from 1 to 12.

crewel or embroidery: These very sharp needles have elongated eyes that can hold strands of embroidery floss or yarn. Sizes range from 1 to 10.

tapestry: These thicker needles have blunt tips and large eyes in sizes 13 to 28. The eye can accept several strands of floss, yarn, or decorative threads. The blunt tip will not damage fabrics.

There also are quite a few types of specialty needles available, including the calyx, a sharp needle with a slot so that the thread can slide down to the needle's eye. These sometimes are called self-threading needles.

....

keep your hand-sewing needles threaded with a short piece of thread when they are stored in a pincushion. They'll be easier to remove that way and you'll never lose one that's been pushed all the way into the pincushion.

....

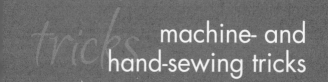

tricks machine- and hand-sewing tricks

machine- and hand-sewing tricks

A creative mess is better than tidy idleness.
—*Anonymous*

to thread a needle, most of us wet the end of the thread. Instead, try wetting the eye of the needle. Just lick the needle—it makes it easier!

....

place the needle in front of a white piece of paper to make the needle eye more visible.

....

needle eyes are punched by machine, and thread will always go through the eye easier from the side it was punched. So, if you're having a hard time threading your needle, turn it around and thread it from the other side (Fig. 10).

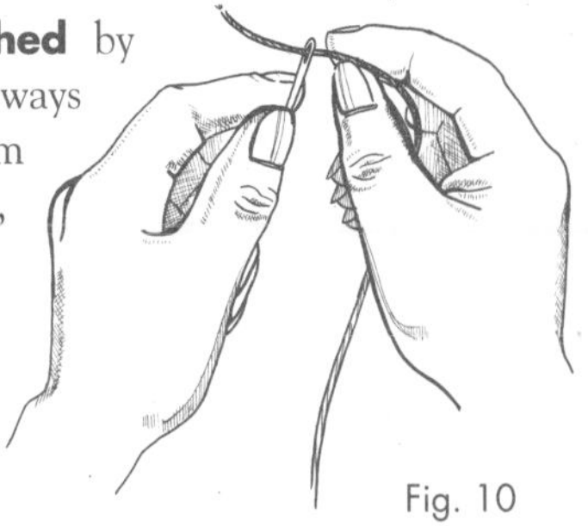

Fig. 10

or, you can use a needle threader (Fig. 11). Slip the wire loop through the eye of a hand needle, feed your thread through the loop, and then pull the loop back out of the eye, bringing the thread with it. Job done.

....

monofilament thread can be difficult to thread through a needle. Mark the tip of the thread with a permanent marker and it's easier to see.

....

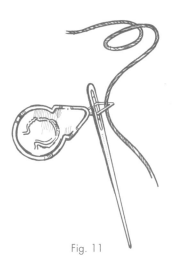

Fig. 11

the quilter's knot is easy (Fig. 12) to make and foolproof. After threading the needle, make a loop with the end that went through the eye, holding the end in place above the needle with your right thumb (A). Wrap the thread around the needle three times (B) and hold it with your thumb as you slide the wraps down the length of the needle, over the eye, and down the length of the thread, ending about a half inch from the end (C). Trim close to the knot. If you want a larger knot, just make more wraps.

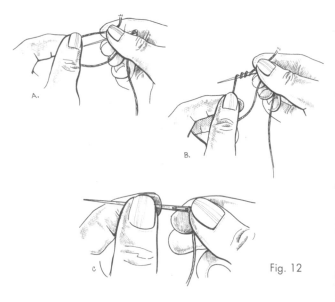

Fig. 12

to keep your hand-sewing thread from tangling, run it through a cake of beeswax from your sewing box. (There are other thread-conditioner products on the market that produce the same results.)

....

to untangle knots in your hand stitching, place your needle through the loop and pull it up. Then put the needle under the knot and pull up until the knot is released (Fig. 13). Pull the thread taut and continue with your stitching.

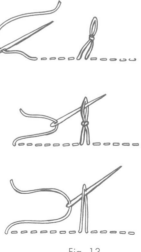

Fig. 13

if you're sewing with a double thread, don't knot the ends together. Knot each end separately and proceed with your sewing. The threads won't tangle together so much.

....

your sewing scissors are to be used for cutting fabric only. Sometimes it's a good idea to hide them from your family, who may not understand the "hands off my scissors" rule. We've even heard of people putting locks on their scissors—which may be a little extreme.

....

scissors blades become dull through use. Sharpen them when they need it. And you might give them the treat of a professional sharpening now and then.

....

don't lay your scissors near the edge of the table when not in use. They can be knocked out of alignment if dropped on the floor.

....

these are some basic hand-sewing stitches you'll find useful. Practice them on a piece of fabric to get the feel of the stitches, and soon you'll be ready to tackle any hand-sewing project.

the running stitch (Fig. 14) is a fast and easy straight stitch that's often used for basting. Insert the needle at evenly spaced intervals into the fabric several times, then pull the needle and thread through the fabric. Repeat as needed. This stitch can be used to gather fabric.

Fig. 14

the backstitch (Fig. 15) is one of the strongest stitches and looks a lot like machine stitching on the front side. It's used for sewing and repairing seams and inserting zippers. To stitch, bring the needle up at 1 and insert behind the starting point at 2. Bring the needle back up at 3. Repeat.

Fig. 15

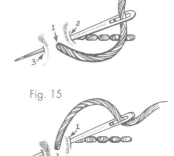

31

the slip stitch (Fig. 16) is used for hand hemming and hand-turned appliqué, and is almost invisible from both sides of the work. It's generally used to join a folded edge to a flat piece of fabric, such as the hem of a skirt. Working from right to left, slip the needle inside the fold for about ¼ inch. Then, pick up a couple of threads from the flat fabric and insert the needle into the fold again. Repeat.

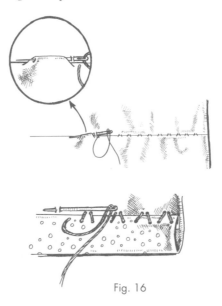

Fig. 16

the catch stitch (Fig. 17) is a hand-hemming stitch used to attach a raw edge (or one with a seam tape sewn on it) to a flat fabric, such as a hem on a skirt. The stitch is nearly invisible from the front side of the fabric but is visible from the back, so it is often used when the project is lined. Working from left to right, insert the needle at 1, pick up a thread or two of the fabric, and bring the needle up at 2. Take the next stitch ¼ inch ahead in the edge and insert it at 3. Pick up a couple of threads and bring the needle back up at 4. Repeat.

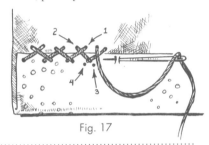

Fig. 17

the blind catch stitch, or blind stitch (Fig. 18), is worked the same way as the catch stitch. The only difference is you will fold back the hem edge about ¼ inch and work between the folded edge and the main fabric. When finished, fold up the edge and the hand stitching will not show.

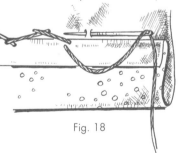

Fig. 18

33

to make a basic finishing knot to end your hand stitching, turn to the back side of your work. Wrap the thread around the needle three times (Fig. 19), and then pull the needle through the wrapped thread to make a knot. Bury the thread under the previous stitches about ½ inch and clip.

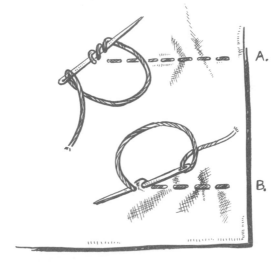

A.

B.

Fig. 19

hooks and eyes (Fig. 20) are used to fasten neckline edges above a zipper or to hold together jacket or sweater edges that meet. Place the eye so that the edge lies just over the garment edge. Use doubled and waxed thread to sew the eye in place using a buttonhole stitch. Slide the needle between the layers and bring it up to stitch the loop in place. Attach the hook to the loop for placement and stitch it in place the same way. Make sure none of your stitches show on the right side.

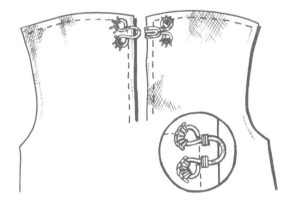

Fig. 20

hooks and bars are used on an overlapping edge such as a waistband (Fig. 21). Place the hook on the back side of the overlap close to the edge. Stitch it in place with a buttonhole stitch. Position the bar and stitch.

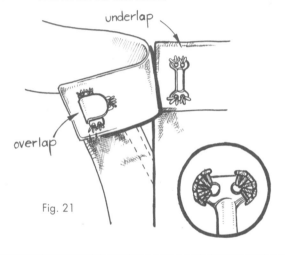

underlap

overlap

Fig. 21

never, ever sew over pins in your fabric. The machine needle can break and get caught in the mechanism. Or the needle can get nicked, causing catches in the fabric. Just remove the pins as you come to them.

some pins have plastic heads that can melt when ironed over. Glass-headed pins are a better choice.

topstitching is a lovely embellishment, but it's often difficult to find a good color match of special topstitching thread. There is a solution. Use two threads of the one used for the garment's regular stitching. Wind thread on a bobbin and place it on the second thread holder on the machine. Thread the two threads (from the spool and the bobbin) through the machine as one and stitch.

store your thread in drawers and covered boxes to prevent dust buildup and fading from sun exposure.

ever had your machine eat up the pieces when you begin to sew? Place a small scrap of fabric under the pressure foot as you begin to feed your sewing under the foot and you'll have no more trouble.

a walking foot walks over the fabric and prevents the upper fabric from sliding over the lower one. It's useful for matching fabric patterns, working with slippery fabric, and preventing knitted fabrics from stretching. It's also an essential tool in quilting (Fig. 22).

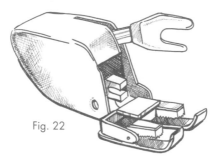

Fig. 22

. . . .

if you are having trouble putting your walking foot on your machine, try lowering the feed dogs. This fraction of an inch will help tremendously. Remember to raise them afterward.

. . . .

sometimes it seems you cannot raise the presser foot high enough to put on the walking foot. Use your knee lift to give you a little more space, and the foot will go on easily.

. . . .

preshrinking eliminates the possibility of fusible interfacing wrinkling (Fig. 23) while it's being fused in place. If the fabric and interfacing haven't been preshrunk before they are cut, the pieces will shrink with the heat and steam from the iron, and generally not at the same rate.

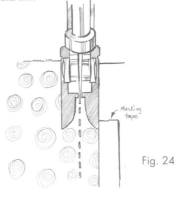

Fig. 23

if the throat plate of your machine isn't marked in inches, place a piece of masking tape or painter's tape (Fig. 24) as a seam guide. Measure from the needle point and add the seam allowance you would like.

Masking tape

Fig. 24

stay-stitching is the secret to keeping garment pieces from stretching as they are being handled (Fig 25). Don't pivot at the corners; cut the thread and start again as shown in the example. Stitch ⅛ inch outside the seam line using a regular stitch length. Don't backstitch. Note that stitching begins and ends at the center of the back and front pieces.

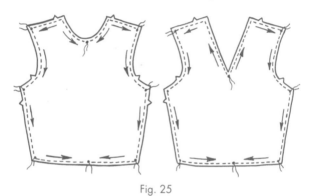

Fig. 25

never stay-stitch long bias edges, as they'll be distorted by the sewing.

if you want to stitch a completely invisible hem in a silk skirt or pants, underline the entire skirt or pants with tulle or the pants with tulle or silk organza. Fold up the hem and hand stitch it by catching only the underlining. Result: No stitches will show on the outside.

....

wash your hands frequently while you are hand stitching. Hot, sweaty hands can make your thread and fabric grimy in a hurry.

....

sit in a comfortable chair with plenty of light behind your left shoulder if you're right-handed or your right shoulder if you're left-handed. Hold the work in your lap. If the project is heavy, sit at a table and let the bulk of the weight rest on the table.

....

lay a clean dish towel across your lap when you're working on a small or medium-sized project and proceed with your sewing. When you need to stop just fold the towel over your work and put it away. It will be ready to pick up and continue whenever you are.

....

it's tempting to work with a long thread, but this can cause tangling and knotting problems. Eighteen inches is a workable length.

. . . .

before starting to hand sew a hem or seam, hold the fabric in place with pins or hand basting.

. . . .

hand stitches should be consistent in their length and regularly spaced for a pleasing effect.

. . . .

a stitch in time saves nine is the number one rule in mending. Fix it right away: Loose buttons get lost, and a small seam rip becomes a disaster.

. . . .

the trick to sewing on a two- or four-hole button securely is creating a thread shank (Fig. 26). Cut a 36-inch thread, double it, and knot it. Secure the knot on the right side of the fabric where the button will be sewn. Position the button and take a stitch up through the hole, then go back through the opposite hole, piercing all the layers. Place a toothpick across the button and take several more stitches. Remove the toothpick, lift the button against the stitches, and you'll see the thread shank. Wrap the thread tightly around the shank four or more times to strengthen the shank. Finish off by taking a few backstitches under the button to secure it.

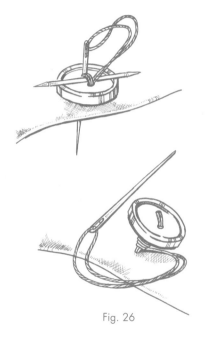

Fig. 26

reinforced buttons (Fig. 27) are used on heavy coats, suits and jackets, and garments made of leather or suede. Place a small flat button on the back of the garment under the

larger button and sew directly from one button to the other, giving added strength. Place a toothpick across the top button to make a shank and take several more stitches. Finish as above.

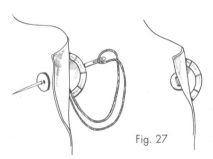

Fig. 27

---

shank buttons can be attached in two ways. Align the shank in the same direction as the buttonhole (Fig. 28). Sew securely by taking small stitches through the shank. If you want the button to be detachable, work a small eyelet using a buttonhole stitch. Push the shank through the eyelet and secure it on the back side of the fabric with a toggle.

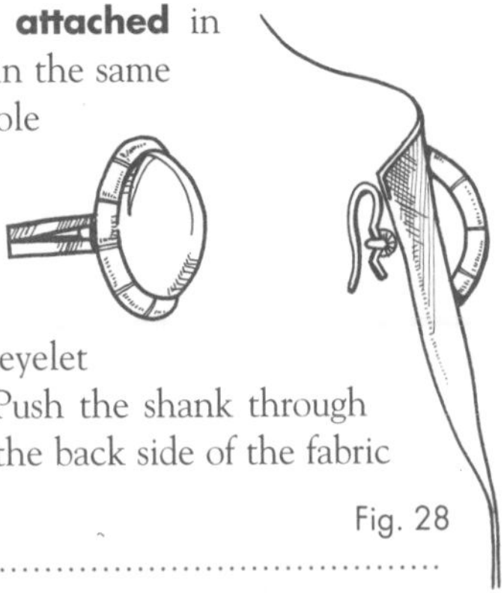

Fig. 28

44

buttons with four eyes can become even more decorative by sewing onto the fabric in various ways. Contrasting thread can make the stitching even more colorful (Fig. 29).

Fig. 29

small puckers that form at the top edge of a hem after it has been hand stitched often can be steamed out. Don't rip out your stitches until you've tried steaming out the puckers.

use binder clips instead of pins to hold fabric pieces together when the fabric could be damaged by pinholes.

keep a lint roller handy in your sewing room to tidy up stray threads on your ironing board and around your chair.

45

before hemming a skirt, dress, or pants, let the garment hang for a day on a hanger to allow the fabric to settle.

....

always hang a bias-cut garment on a padded hanger for at least forty-eight hours before hemming. This gives the fabric a chance to relax. If the garment is hemmed without hanging first, you'll end up with a distorted hemline. A narrow hem works best for a bias design.

....

good old clothes that have become tired or have gone out of style can be revived for a second life, and in today's world that just makes good sense.

....

a frayed collar or cuffs can be restored by adding a contrasting binding or hand embroidery in a close buttonhole stitch.

....

try dyeing a faded garment that's made of an all-natural material such as cotton or linen.

....

it is easier to change a garment into another by cutting away rather than adding on. A pair of pants can become a skirt, not the other way around.

....

restyling a dress can be as creative as making a new one, plus it's easy since most of the seams are already sewn.

....

the neckline of a dress or top with a jewel neckline can easily be changed. Face the new neckline with a coordinating fabric.

....

pants with worn knees can easily by restyled into shorts. If the original pants had no pockets, patch pockets can be cut from the pant legs.

....

all about patterns

all about patterns

> I was cut out to be RICH;
> I was just sewn up wrong.
> —*Anonymous*

ebenezer butterick changed the face of home sewing forever by creating the first graded sewing pattern in 1863. Butterick's innovation was offering every pattern in a series of standard, graded sizes. Before then, patterns came in one size only and it was up to the sewer to make the pattern fit. His first efforts were cardboard templates for men's and boy's clothing. By experimenting he found that tissue paper was much lighter, foldable, and easier to send by mail.

. . . .

place your pattern pieces on the fabric following the layout. Pin by placing the pins (Fig. 30) perpendicular to the seam lines with the pinheads pointing to the inside. Place a pin every 3 to 4 inches.

. . . .

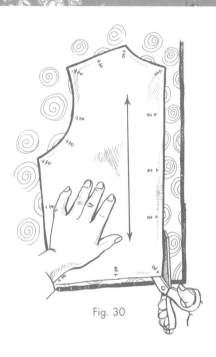

Fig. 30

keep the entire pin within the pattern boundary. By doing this you'll avoid cutting the pins with your scissors and damaging the blades. If you're pinning a delicate fabric, keep the pin entrance and exit within the seam allowance.

pattern weights can be used instead of pins (Fig. 31) to hold a paper pattern in place on the fabric for cutting. Most any small heavy object can be used, such as lead fishing weights, smooth rocks, or rolled coins, or you can buy packaged weights at your local fabric shop.

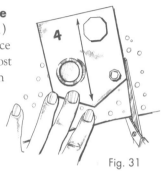

Fig. 31

why use weights? Some fabrics such as leathers would be damaged by pinholes. Other fabrics are just too heavy to pin.

the major pattern companies generally print separate patterns for each size. Many of the smaller companies and European companies manufacture multisize patterns (Fig. 32) with all the sizes superimposed on one another. Some patterns use different graphic patterns of dashes, dots, and lines for each size. Once you find your size, use a highlighter to mark your size for each pattern piece. This saves a lot of confusion.

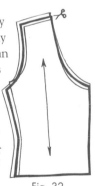

Fig. 32

you can cut your highlighted pattern pieces directly. If you want to preserve the whole pattern, trace off your size onto the material of your choice.

....

some multisize patterns do not include seam allowances so make this determination before you cut out your fabric.

....

some sewers like to use favorite patterns again and again. One way to preserve a pattern is to iron it onto lightweight fusible interfacing then cut it out. Press the tissue pattern pieces with a dry iron first to remove all the folds and wrinkles. Be sure to preshrink the fusible interfacing before fusing.

....

another way to preserve a tissue pattern is to first press the pattern pieces with a dry iron and then press the wrong side of the pattern to the shiny side of freezer paper. Cut out the pieces and store.

....

yet another material to trace a pattern onto is painter's clear plastic drop cloth, which is available in rolls from home-improvement and hardware stores. Use a fine-point marker to trace the pattern pieces and then cut them out. Be sure to trace the grain lines and add the pattern number and other pertinent information. Choose a medium-weight plastic.

....

have you noticed that the sizes of ready-to-wear clothing are different from sewing pattern sizes? Ready-to-wear began giving smaller sizes to larger clothing in the 1930s, a practice called vanity sizing. Pattern companies tried to keep up with the ready-to-wear industry's changing size designations. By the 1970s, however, the pattern industry stopped changing pattern sizes. A pattern purchased today has the same sizing as a pattern from the '70s.

....

cut out the pattern accurately. If you are right-handed, place your left hand on the pattern (this will keep the pattern from shifting) and cut with your right hand starting on the right side. This way your cutting hand won't obscure the pattern.

....

don't cut around the notches on the pattern edges. Cut right through them, then go back and make ⅛-inch snip marks at the notches using sharp scissors. Also, snip-mark hemlines, fold lines, and dart lines that appear at the cut edges.

interior marks on the pattern can be transferred by several methods: tailor tacks, pin marking, or using dressmaker's carbon and a tracing wheel.

read your pattern envelope. The front will show a photograph or drawing of the garment along with style variations. A photograph gives a more accurate view of how the finished garment will look on a real person. The size is printed whether it is a multisize, single size, or a small size range (6–8–10, for example). A short description of the style is shown. Any notions required are listed, as are suggestions for suitable fabrics and/or fabric requirements. The back views are shown as small line drawings. Additional specific information regarding the fit and style of the garment often is listed along with the skill level required.

generally, it's a bad idea to use a fabric that has a different weight or drape than those suggested on the pattern envelope. Never use a woven fabric for a pattern designed for knit fabrics only.

....

fabric layout guides are included with the pattern. The layout will include all the pattern pieces needed with an illustration of how to lay them on the fabric. It also will show if the pattern is cut from a single layer or double layers of fabric.

....

if you find a pattern in a style you've never worn and you're not sure how it will look on you, go shopping. Try on a similar garment in ready-to-wear and you'll find out in a hurry if it is flattering to you. It's discouraging to spend the time and money to make something that doesn't suit you.

....

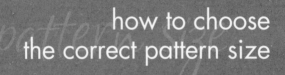

how to choose
the correct pattern size

how to choose the correct pattern size

Friendships are sewn one stitch at a time.
—Anonymous

custom fit begins with accurate body measurements. You'll need these to choose the correct size pattern.

....

first, measure your body (Fig. 33). Remember to wear your normal undergarments when measuring, making sure your bra fits well and the straps are adjusted correctly. Tie a piece of narrow elastic around your waist, settling it where you bend at the side. Use a nonstretching measuring tape and make sure it is held snug and taut (but not tightly) against your body and is parallel to the floor. Record these measurements and the date and update them every six months or so, or anytime you've had a change in weight.

....

high bust: Measure straight across the back and around the body above the fullest part of the bust (1).

....

full bust: Measure around the fullest part of the bust (2).

....

waist: Measure around the body at the natural waistline (3).

....

Fig. 33

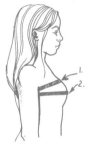

hip: Measure around the body at the fullest part—usually 7 to 9 inches below the waist (4).

....

center back: Measure from the prominent neck bone to the waist.

....

height: Measure (without shoes) standing against a wall.

....

1. chest
high bust

2. full bust

3. waistline

4. full hip

select your size category. Compare your height and body measurements to the measurement charts on the pattern envelope to select your size category.

select your pattern size. Pattern size is determined by your measurements, not your ready-to-wear size. Refer to the measurement charts to select the size corresponding to the bust, waist, and hip measurements closest to your measurements. Seldom do we match these numbers exactly. Here are some hints for making the choice.

- For dresses, blouses, tops, vests, jackets, and coats, select the size to correspond with your full bust measurement. Adjust the waist and/or hip if necessary. If there is more than a 2-inch difference between your high bust and full bust measurement, select the pattern size by your high bust measurement, as you'll have a better fit through your shoulders, chest, and upper back. Adjust the full bust if necessary.

- When buying a pattern that includes a blouse, jacket, skirt, and/or pants, choose the size by your full bust measurement and adjust the hip and/or waist if necessary.

- For skirts, pants, and shorts, choose the size to correspond with your waist measurement. Adjust the hip if necessary. If your hips are much larger than your waist, choose the size closest to your hip measurement and adjust the waist.

- If your measurements fall between two sizes, consider your bone structure. If you are thin and small-boned, choose the smaller of the two sizes. If you are larger boned, choose the larger size. Personal preference may also influence your size selection depending on whether you prefer a looser or a closer fit.

- For maternity patterns, select according to your measurements before pregnancy.

....

some patterns now have multisize bodice pieces available by cup size to help with a better fit.

....

to determine your cup size you will need both the full bust measurement and the high bust measurement. Subtract the high bust from the full bust measurements for the difference. Using this *difference* number, find your cup size on the chart on page 62.

....

Cup Size Chart

Difference	Cup Size
Up to 1 inch	A
Up to 2 inches	B
Up to 3 inches	C
Up to 4 inches (10 cm)	D

make it fit

make it fit

> There is no such thing as a screwup in sewing.
> There are only design opportunities
> —*Anonymous*

a croquis is a head-to-toe silhouette drawing of your body. Sketches of various clothing designs can be superimposed over this to help you decide if a design is suited to you.

. . . .

making a croquis is a simple project. The hardest part is having your picture taken in your underwear. Ask a friend or spouse to take a full-length digital photo of you in your undergarments, or maybe you can find a way to take it yourself. Blow it up to full-page size, then trace your outline onto another piece of paper and make copies. There's your croquis. If you're computer savvy, this all can be done at your keyboard.

. . . .

wearing ease is the extra room added to most garments to give you space to move, bend, and sit comfortably. Some styles made from highly stretchable fabric may have negative ease, as the fabric will stretch with you.

....

the back of the pattern envelope describes the fit of the garment, which will give you an idea of the design ease built into the pattern. The chart below gives you an idea of the extra room built into various silhouettes.

Description from pattern envelope	Dress, shirt, vest at full bust	Skirt, slacks, shirt, shorts at hip	Jacket at full bust/chest	Coat
Close fitting	0–3 inches	0–2 inches	envelope	envelope
Fitted	3–4 inches	2–3 inches	envelope	envelope
Semifitted	4–5 inches	3–4 inches	envelope	envelope
Loose fitting	5–8 inches	envelope	envelope	envelope
Very loose fitting	Over 8 inches	envelope	envelope	envelope

YOUR MOST IMPORTANT SEWING TOOL:
A PERFECTLY FITTED MUSLIN

one of the reasons we sew is to have better fitting clothes than can be found off the rack. And the way to achieve that fit is by sewing a muslin fitting shell. Butterick has a fitting shell pattern in misses and misses plus sizes. Detailed instructions help you create a perfect fit. Once all the changes are made and transferred to the tissue pattern, preserve the pattern using your favorite method. Now, when you begin a sewing project you can easily make adjustments to the new pattern using the fitting shell pieces.

when pinning a garment together with the seam allowances to the outside, to check the fit, pin along the seam line like mock stitching. You'll then be able to check the fit from the right side.

if you are using an expensive fabric, sew a muslin working pattern to refine the fit before cutting into the fabric. This muslin copy is called a toile, and taking the time to make it can save costly mistakes. Sew the muslin pieces together with the machine basting stitch. These stitches will be easier to remove when fitting.

making a muslin toile is a good idea when working with a challenging pattern. All the kinks can be worked out before cutting into the fabric.

....

start the fitting from the shoulder seams and work your way down, adjusting one seam at a time with pins, rebasting, and trying it on again. Transfer all the corrections to the paper pattern in pencil. After all the revisions are made, the muslin fits perfectly, and the grain lines hang straight, ink in and tape down the revisions to the paper pattern.

....

it's all about
the fabric

it's all about the fabric

One yard of fabric, like one cookie, is never enough!
—Anonymous

isn't it annoying to have to unfold fabrics in your stash to find one with the yardage you need for a sewing project? Here's how to put an end to that problem. Measure and refold each fabric. Place a piece of painter's tape on the top corner and mark it with the yardage. Problem solved.

....

when you're considering fabrics to buy, take a few steps back and look at the fabrics again. They can look very different from this view.

....

take your fabric selections to a window, or better yet, go outside. Artificial light can make the colors look very different.

....

if you don't know the fiber content of a piece of fabric, try the burn test (Fig. 34) to identify the fiber. Cut a small swatch of the fabric, hold it with tongs, and light it with a match either outdoors or over a sink. Watch how it burns and how the residue looks.

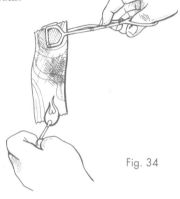

Fig. 34

....

cotton and linen are vegetable fibers. They catch fire easily and burn well. The ash is easily crumbled.

....

wool and silk are protein fibers that do not catch fire easily. They smell like burning hair and leave a crumbling ash.

....

71

viscose rayon and acetate are made from cellulose. Viscose rayon burns well and leaves little ash. Acetate burns well and the remaining ash is hard.

....

nylon, acrylic, and polyester are coal/oil/petroleum products that burn easily and leave a black bead of residue or hard ash.

....

a metric meter is 39.37 inches.

....

it's tempting to use the selvage edge of the fabric as it's tightly woven and has a finished edge. Don't do it as it can distort the finished seam. Cut it off and discard it.

....

when cutting pattern pieces for a bias design, do not fold the fabric to cut through two layers at once. Cut each piece from a single layer, being sure to flip duplicate pieces when necessary. For instance, if you are cutting a left skirt front, you must flip over the pattern to cut the right skirt front.

....

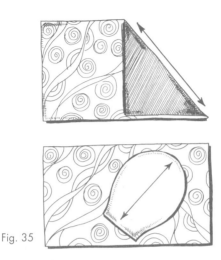

Fig. 35

when a design calls for fabric to be cut on the bias, you first need to find the true bias. After straightening the fabric, place it on a flat surface and make a diagonal fold (Fig. 35). The diagonally folded edge is the true bias. Handle the fabric carefully, as fabrics will stretch when pulled across the grain. Place the pattern pieces on the true bias using the grain-line marking on the pattern as a guide.

select mostly midweight fabrics for garments that can be worn for most of the year. And, most importantly, choose a suitable fabric for the design.

· ·

when working with a fabric you've never used before, experiment with some scraps. If you want to use a special technique such as pleats, try it out on spare fabric before you make the commitment of cutting out the pattern.

· ·

when you select a fabric to purchase, make a note of the fiber content and care instructions from the end of the bolt. Transfer this information to your sewing journal.

· ·

if you are cutting a slippery fabric, you need a nonslip surface. Spread a flat cotton sheet over the cutting surface, and your slipping problems will be solved.

· ·

if you have table pads for your dining room table, put them on your table upside down. The flannel side will keep fabrics from sliding and you will have just created a large cutting surface.

· ·

press as you go!

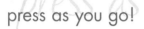

press as you go!

Sewing fills my days, not to mention the living
room, bedrooms, and closets.

—Anonymous

the number one rule in sewing is to press as you sew. This makes such a difference in your finished product—the difference between "handmade" and the dreaded "homemade" look.

....

the number one rule in pressing is not to rush.

....

proper pressing is not the same as ironing. When ironing the iron is moved back and forth continuously on the fabric. When pressing, the iron is set down, then lifted up and moved to the next spot.

....

set up your pressing equipment near your sewing machine and use it constantly as you sew. If you wait until the project is finished, it will be too late to get that high-end ready-made look.

....

never cross a seam with another (such as attaching a bodice to a skirt) until the first seam has been properly pressed.

your two major pressing purchases are your ironing board and your iron. Buy the best your budget allows.

buy an adjustable height ironing board. It's a whole lot more comfortable when the board can be adjusted to your height. Plus, there may be times when you'll want to sit at the board.

boards vary in size. If you have the storage space, buy a long, wide one. You'll find a large surface useful.

cover your board with extra padding if it has only a thin layer over the mesh top.

make sure your cover is 100 percent cotton. The Teflon-coated covers are not recommended when you're sewing, as they reflect heat back into the fabric, which can cause shine and problems with fusing.

an iron is an iron is an iron doesn't hold true. You'll want a steam iron that produces heavy steam, has a smooth soleplate, and doesn't spit.

⋯⋯⋯⋯⋯⋯⋯⋯⋯⋯⋯⋯⋯⋯⋯⋯⋯⋯⋯⋯⋯⋯⋯⋯⋯⋯⋯

another choice is a tank iron that has a separate water reservoir and produces a higher volume of steam.

⋯⋯⋯⋯⋯⋯⋯⋯⋯⋯⋯⋯⋯⋯⋯⋯⋯⋯⋯⋯⋯⋯⋯⋯⋯⋯⋯

use the correct temperature for your fabric. Your iron doesn't need to be at its highest temperature to produce good steam.

⋯⋯⋯⋯⋯⋯⋯⋯⋯⋯⋯⋯⋯⋯⋯⋯⋯⋯⋯⋯⋯⋯⋯⋯⋯⋯⋯

press cloths are used when pressing all fabrics except cotton and linen to prevent shine and protect your fabric from the heat and imprint of the iron.

⋯⋯⋯⋯⋯⋯⋯⋯⋯⋯⋯⋯⋯⋯⋯⋯⋯⋯⋯⋯⋯⋯⋯⋯⋯⋯⋯

you can use any smoothly woven natural fabric as a press cloth. Muslin cut to 12 by 18 inches and pinked around the edges makes a good cloth. An undyed cotton or linen dish towel works well. Or, cut a press cloth from an old 100 percent cotton sheet. Generally, a wool press cloth is used when pressing heavy wool.

⋯⋯⋯⋯⋯⋯⋯⋯⋯⋯⋯⋯⋯⋯⋯⋯⋯⋯⋯⋯⋯⋯⋯⋯⋯⋯⋯

use a sports water bottle to fill your steam iron's water reservoir. The water will pour directly into the reservoir with no drips.

. . . .

a tailor's ham and seam roll are two very useful pressing tools (Fig. 36). Both are firmly stuffed and covered with wool on one half and heavy cotton on the other. Use the side that most closely matches your fabric.

. . . .

the tailor's ham is used to press darts and shaped seams to preserve their contours. If pressed flat, you'll have a garment without shape.

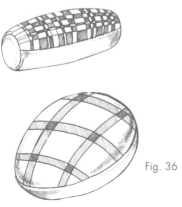

Fig. 36

to press a dart, first press it flat to meld the stitches into the fabric. Then slide the fabric over the ham to the spot the dart hugs best. Press the dart on the wrong side from the wide end to the narrow (Fig. 37).

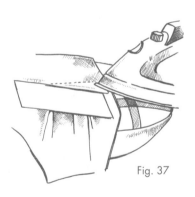

Fig. 37

darts in heavier fabrics (Fig. 38) can be slashed open to eliminate bulk. Cut the dart through the middle within ½ inch of the point and press open. On wide darts press the point flat. On narrow darts press the point to one side.

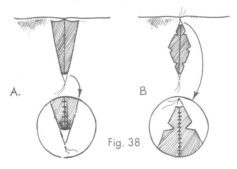

Fig. 38

....

a seam roll makes it easy to press tubular pieces such as sleeves and pants legs.

....

improvise a seam roll by tightly rolling up a terry cloth towel.

....

if you're not using a seam roll, strips of brown paper (or computer paper or adding machine tape) can be slipped under the seam allowance to avoid seam imprints.

....

generally, bodice and skirt darts are pressed toward one another. Bust darts are pressed downward (Fig. 39).

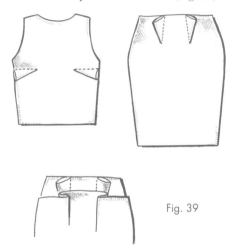

Fig. 39

press in the same direction you stitched. This avoids stretching and distortion.

never press over pins or basting stitches, as they can imprint on the fabric. Also, pins with plastic heads can melt, and that could be disastrous.

to press a seam, lay the piece flat on the ironing board. Press along the line of stitching in the direction sewn to set the stitches into the fabric. Open up the two pieces of fabric and place them over a seam roll. Use the tip of the iron and your fingers to open the seam and direct the steam into the fabric (Fig. 40). Make sure you are pressing in a straight line and not distorting the seam. Flip over the seam and press from the right side, using a press cloth if the fabric requires it.

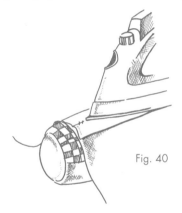

Fig. 40

let the freshly pressed item cool on the ironing board before moving it. This helps it keep its shape.

the custom touch

the custom touch

> May your bobbin always be full.
> —*Anonymous*

literally translated, the French term "haute couture" means sewing at a higher level. Surprisingly, most of the techniques used in couture workrooms can be duplicated at home. Couture garments are custom cut and carefully fitted to the few individuals who can afford them. But isn't that exactly what we as home sewers are doing? What we often do not do is take our sewing to the higher level.

....

the inside of our garments should look as good as the outside, and that easily is accomplished by finishing the seams. Keeping the edges from raveling also is a safety measure.

....

the pinked seam is the easiest seam finish (Fig. 41). This is practical for a firmly woven fabric. For the most secure finish, stitch ¼ inch from each seam edge, then cut away the fabric outside the stitching with pinking shears. Or you can pink the seam edges without the stitching.

86

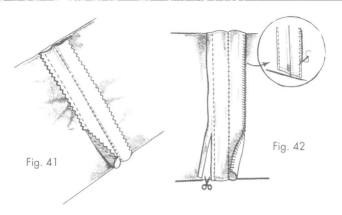

Fig. 41

Fig. 42

the hand overcast finish (Fig. 42) is suitable for most fabrics. Stitch ⅛ inch from the edge of the seam, then hand overcast the edge using the machine stitch as a guide.

. . . .

the turned under seam (Fig. 43) is best used for lightweight fabrics and plain weave synthetics. Turn under the raw edges of the seam allowances, press if necessary, and stitch close to the edge.

. . . .

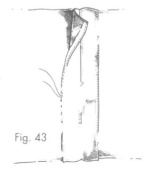

Fig. 43

the bound edge (Fig. 44) is used for bulky and easily raveled fabrics. Encase each raw edge in purchased double-fold bias tape. The slightly narrower edge of the tape is placed on top and edge-stitched.

....

the zigzag edge (Fig. 45) is stitched close to but not over the raw edge of the seam allowance. Set a long stitch length and a wide stitch. If the zigzag runs over the edge it can cause tunneling, and the seam will not lie flat.

Fig. 44

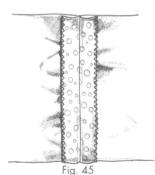

Fig. 45

the hong kong finish (Fig. 46) gives the best look for unlined garments. Cut bias strips 1½ inches wide from a lining type fabric that blends with the garment fabric. Sew these strips to the garment seam allowance in a ⅛-inch seam, right sides of fabric facing. Press the lining fabric away from the seam. Wrap the lining fabric to the back side, enclosing the raw edge. Stitch in the ditch to complete. If there is excess lining fabric on the back side, trim it away.

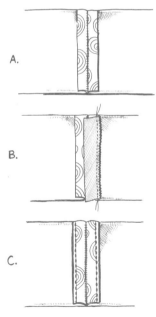

A.

B.

C.

Fig. 46

couture is a combination of fine fabrics and fine detailing using the finest craftsmanship. Detailing can be visible, such as pleats and tucks, or invisible, such as an underlining that ensures a proper fit. It's an attention to detail that means you spend more time working with your hands than stitching at the machine. The rewards of these custom techniques are immeasurable.

....

the prick stitch is used to hand insert a zipper. The technique is basically the same as the backstitch; however, the spacing is different.

1. Insert the needle up from the back side of the fabric ¹⁄₁₆ inch from the right edge and pull it through.

2. Insert the needle to the right three or four threads and bring it out ¼ inch to the left of the previous stitch.

3. Continue stitching, smoothing the fabric every few stitches. End with a fastening stitch, catching only the underneath part of the fabric.

nothing sets apart a garment as custom made more than a lining or underlining. An underlining gives support to the garment. It is cut in the shapes of the main pieces and sewn to each piece of the garment. The two layers then are treated as one during construction. A lining is constructed separately and is installed inside the garment as a layer to separate the garment from the body. This keeps the garment from clinging and also serves to finish the inside, concealing construction details.

EMBELLISHMENT: MAKING IT YOUR OWN

even the slightest additions of trim or ornament can add a strong personal accent to your clothes.

---

tie a brightly colored silk scarf around the waist of a neutral dress or sew a braided trim down a pants leg, and an outfit will go from bland to wow.

---

throughout most of history, the fabrics chosen for clothing, the style, the trim, and even the accessories worn were governed by stern rules. These regulations—known as sumptuary laws—were designed to prevent extravagance by the common people.

---

braids, rickrack, ribbons, soutache, fringe, tassels, pompons, beading, and embroidery are readily available trims that can transform a garment by adding color and character.

. . . .

fabric stores generally carry a limited supply of trims. Mail order sources are your best bet for finding a wide variety of styles and colors.

. . . .

grosgrain ribbon has a ribbed texture and comes in a wide range of widths and colors. Stitch several rows at the bottom edge of a skirt, or stitch a row down each side seam of a pair of summer slacks.

. . . .

rickrack has a distinctive zigzag shape and is available in many widths and colors. It can be used to trim casual clothing and children's clothes as well as household items.

. . . .

machine sewing is the fast and easy way to apply trims. The key to success with machine sewing is choosing the right pressure foot for the job. For sewing narrow cords and trims, the pressure foot must have a hole, slot, or groove that holds the trim as it feeds beneath the pressure foot. The size of the hole, slot, or groove should match the size of the trim as accurately as possible.

wide trims can be applied with an adjustable zipper foot, edge-stitch foot, or a standard zigzag foot. The needle positions on the machine should be adjusted to stitch accurately along the edge of the trim.

a simple Kmart t-shirt can be changed into a boutique-style work of art using any of these trims. Give it a try and have a good time playing. It's sort of like finger painting—anything goes.

use your sewing machine twin needle to sew down a narrow ribbon. Make sure the ribbon is just a little wider than the spacing between the two needles. It results in a much neater look than sewing each side separately, as the spacing between the two rows will be perfect.

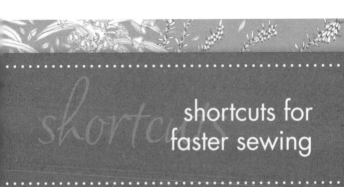

shortcuts for
faster sewing

shortcuts for faster sewing

Old seamstresses never go crazy;
they just stay on pins and needles.
—*Anonymous*

It's really annoying when spools of thread start unwinding
on their own. Here's an easy way to put a stop to it. Unwind 6
inches of thread. Wrap the thread around the spool one time,
catching your finger under the thread. Thread the end under
the loop made by your finger (Fig. 47), remove your finger, and
pull the thread taut. You've created a slipknot. The thread still
can be pulled off the spool, but it will not unwind on its own.

Fig. 47

To create a continuous bias binding strip:

1. Cut the fabric square in half diagonally. Place the two triangle pieces right sides together with the straight edges on the right (Fig. 48). Press the seam open.

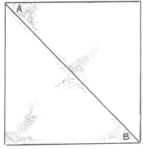
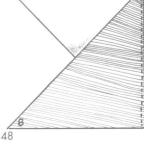

Fig. 48

2. Using a transparent gridded ruler, draw a parallel line every 2¼ inches (or width needed) on the wrong side of the fabric (Fig. 49).

Fig. 49

3. Fold the marked piece right sides together to form a tube, aligning the edges and pinning the marked lines so one width of the binding extends beyond the edge on each side, as shown in

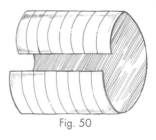

Fig. 50

Fig. 50. Sew the tube together with a ¼-inch seam. Press the seam open. Cut on the marked line to make one continuous 2¼-inch-wide bias binding strip.

. . . .

stop your machine foot pedal from scooting around on tile or wooden floors. Just place a piece of Rubbermaid drawer liner underneath it and it'll stay put.

. . . .

a small piece of this handy drawer liner placed by your machine will corral your scissors and other small tools, keeping them from rolling off your sewing table.

. . . .

a piece under your sewing machine will keep it steady on your sewing surface.

. . . .

sew longer and have better posture by placing two doorstops under the back of your machine to raise it 1 inch. It's amazing how much better you'll feel after a long sewing session.

....

take a break. Get up from your sewing chair (whether you're at your machine or doing hand stitching) and walk around the room every half hour or so. Do some neck and shoulder rolls. You'll feel better for it.

....

a simple way to stop your foot pedal from wandering as you sew is to just put more of your foot on the pedal. The weight of your heel resting on the pedal instead of the floor will keep you from pushing the pedal away as you sew.

....

the easiest and least damaging way to remove stitches is with a seam ripper (Fig. 51). Cut every third stitch, and then cover the line with masking tape. Turn the seam over and pull away the thread on the other side. Turn it back over and remove the masking tape. All the loose threads will come off with the tape.

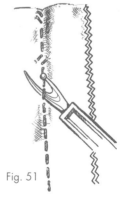

Fig. 51

....

the loose threads can also be removed with tweezers.

....

recycling is the name of the game. If you have clothing that is beyond donating for a second life, remove any usable zippers, buttons, or decorative trim and add them to your stash.

....

if clothing you are donating has "killer" buttons, remove them and replace them with appropriate buttons.

....

sometimes clothing will have wonderful fabric but an "unfixable" stain or tear. Cut it up! Fabric from a dress can become a beautiful top.

....

deciding on the right zipper for a project can sometimes be confusing. Here is bit of information on the different types of zippers (Fig. 52).

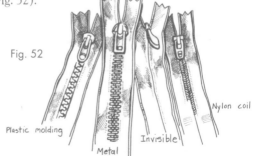

Fig. 52

Plastic molding

Metal

Invisible

Nylon coil

metal zippers have two lines of metal teeth that have been molded and placed on either side of the tape at regular intervals. The teeth can be made from aluminum, nickel, or brass. They are most commonly found on jeans.

....

plastic molded zippers are the same as metal zippers except the teeth have been molded out of plastic.

....

invisible zippers most often are used in dresses and skirts. The coil on an invisible zipper is located on the back side of the zipper and will not be visible from the front of a garment after the zipper has been installed. Invisible zippers are usually coil zippers with a teardrop pull.

....

nylon coil zippers are the most common type of zippers. They used to be made from nylon and are still commonly referred to as nylon coil zippers even though now they are typically made from polyester. Coil zippers are lightweight, heat resistant, and rustproof.

....

separating zippers (Fig. 53) are designed so the two sides of the tape are able to come apart completely after the zipper has been installed. Separating zippers use a box and pin mechanism. They are most commonly found on coats and sweatshirts.

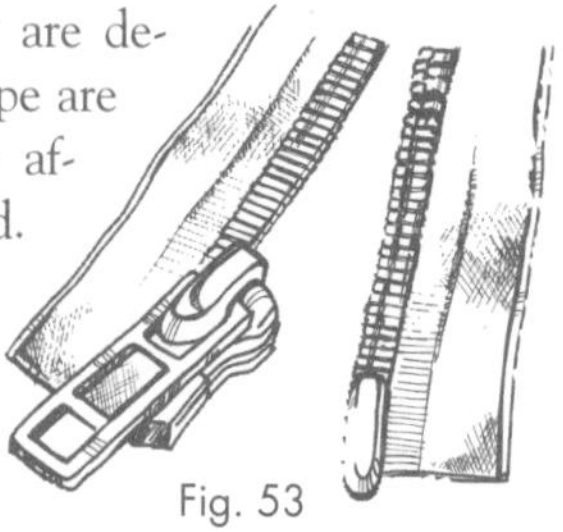

Fig. 53

anatomy of a zipper (Fig. 54): There are three major parts to every zipper: the tape, the slider, and the teeth. When the two sides of teeth are joined it creates the chain.

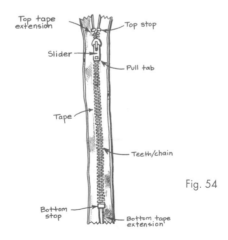

Top tape extension

Top stop

Slider

Pull tab

Tape

Teeth/chain

Bottom stop

Bottom tape extension

Fig. 54

zippers come in a variety of lengths, but there may be times when you would like to shorten a zipper (Fig. 55). Just stitch over the coils a few times where you want the new stop to be. Cut off the end of the zipper ½ to 1 inch below your newly sewn stop. Any regular scissors will easily cut through the nylon coil.

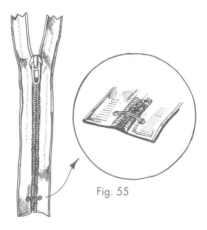

Fig. 55

always launder garments with the zipper closed. When ironing, close the zipper with the slider in place and make sure it is covered with fabric.

103

to unstick a metal zipper, rub the metal teeth with the tip of a pencil, then move the slide up and down a few times.

....

a little liquid soap applied to a stuck zipper can also help.

....

to keep scissors from damaging other items in your sewing basket, cover the points with the rubber protectors sold for knitting needles.

....

a bar of soap makes a great pincushion. In addition to storing pins and needles, it lubricates the tips so that they will slide easily through stiff fabrics. Choose a good-smelling soap to freshen up your sewing area. Be sure to keep it on a soap dish or saucer.

....

there often are faster and simpler ways to sew a garment than the pattern directions may dictate. For instance, setting a sleeve to the bodice flat, and then sewing the underarm seam of the sleeve along with the side seam of the bodice speeds up construction. As long as all of the seams on a garment are sewn to the pattern specifications, it will fit and wear the same. The order of construction makes no difference.

....

it isn't necessary to have long periods of time to sew. It's amazing what can be accomplished in just ten, twenty, or thirty minutes at a time. Maybe in one segment you'll just press; in another stitch a few seams. Before you know it you've finished a project without dedicating hours at a time.

....

set aside time for a cutting marathon. Choose two or three projects, lay out the fabrics and patterns, and cut away. Complete all the necessary marking and you will have several projects ready to sew when you have a few minutes. Fold the fabric pieces for each project over a hanger so they won't wrinkle and group them together in the order you will sew.

....

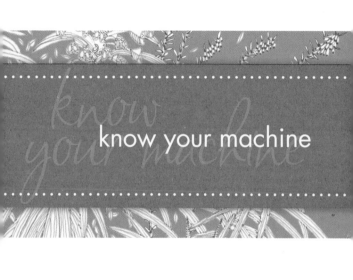

know your machine

know your machine

Behind every sewer is a huge pile of fabric.
—*Anonymous*

read your sewing machine manual from cover to cover. You'll find the answers to most of your questions about your machine.

....

don't have a manual? First contact your local dealer. If that's not possible, find the manufacturer's Web site. You may be able to download a PDF file. If it's a vintage machine, check out eBay. Vintage manuals often are up for bid. Just be sure to have the model number available.

....

have you used all the special feet that came with your machine? It's time to sit down and play. Just grab a half-yard of fabric you're not in love with or an old sheet or piece of muslin and try them all. The manual will tell you how. You'll be absolutely amazed how they can enhance your sewing.

....

if your machine has built-in stitches, use them. Many are functional and can enhance your sewing, and the purely decorative stitches are fun, too. Take a little time to just sit down and play with the stitches and learn what they can do for you. It isn't necessary to have a project; just stitch away.

now that you've used your machine's feet and built-in stitches, make a sampler. Choose a light-colored closely woven material and a dark thread for contrast. Stitch each of the built-in stitches using various lengths and width where applicable. On a separate piece of material use the feet; apply a cord, attach braid, make a buttonhole. Now you have a permanent record of what you and your machine can accomplish.

plug your machine into a good-quality surge protector to protect it from power surges and lightening. Turn off your machine and the breaker on the surge protector when it's not being used.

depending on your sewing setup, when you're not using your machine, either put it back in its protective cover and store it or make sure it's covered with a fabric cover if you leave it out. This will keep dust, dirt, pet hairs, and other airborne gunk from getting into it. Now you have a good excuse to make a cover.

how a sewing machine stitch is formed: A stitch begins when the needle penetrates the fabric and descends to its lowest point. The bobbin hook then slides by the needle's scarf (the indentation at the back of the needle), catches the upper thread, and carries it around the bobbin and bobbin thread (Fig. 56). The thread is then pulled up into the fabric, completing the stitch (Fig. 57).

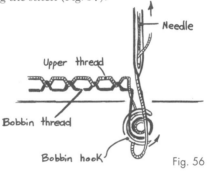

Needle

Upper thread

Bobbin thread

Bobbin hook

Fig. 56

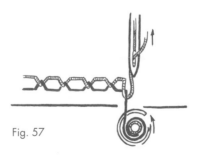

Fig. 57

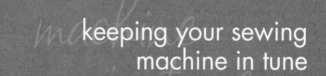

keeping your sewing machine in tune

keeping your sewing machine in tune

Stitch your stress away.
— *Anonymous*

Textile artist and designer Rob Appell shares his hands-on knowledge of sewing machine maintenance to help us keep our machines running in tip-top shape. For more information, go to www.robappell.com.

here are a few things that you can and should do for your sewing machine on a regular basis. Please keep in mind that every sewing machine should be seen by a professional for a full-service call every two or three years; five years is way too long between professional services. Also, the older the machine, the more regularly you should use it. Machine oil and lubricant (white grease) will dry up if the working parts of the machines are not put to use. Even if you do not have a project to work on, it is a good idea to run your machine at least five minutes per month. This may be done without thread, needle, or bobbin. You simply need to keep the lubricants moving through the machine.

Here are a few things you may do often:

1. **use good-quality** thread and needles.

2. **change your needle** after every few hours of use, and try to use the proper needle for the job. A wide variety of needle choices are available, and your dealer will be happy to educate you on the different reasons to pick different needles.

3. **oil your hook.** The hook is the part of the machine that rotates around the bobbin and bobbin case. The hook picks up the thread from behind the needle's eye and wraps it around your bobbin. You should dust out the lint from around the hook, remove the bobbin, and drop one or two drops of oil in the part of the hook that moves around the basket (the part that holds the bobbin and bobbin case). This should be done after you have used about five bobbins of thread. If you're on a sewing marathon, once a day is enough.

4. **clean your feed dogs.** Your sewing machine was not manufactured with little felt pads between the feed dogs—that is, the lint from hours of sewing fun (Fig. 58). You should remove your needle and presser foot, and then remove your stitch plate. Most stitch plates will lift up with slight pressure from between the

113

machine body and the plate itself. Many older machines have one or two flathead screws that hold down the plate from the top. Use a very short-handled screwdriver to loosen these screws. My favorite mini screwdriver has little wings on the handle so that I can apply a good amount of pressure even though it's a small handle (Fig. 59). Once the plate is off, dust out the space between the feed dogs. If you think of the feed dogs as teeth, then you are flossing the gums of the feed dogs. The more accumulated lint you have, the less lift there is on the feed system, and the poorer the quality of your stitch.

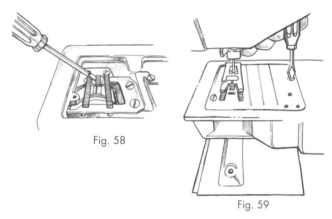

Fig. 58

Fig. 59

5. **last, but most important,** never use cans of "spray air" or "air duster." These products are propelled by compressed gas and will blast moisture into your machine and make mud out of the lint you were trying to remove. It's best to use a nylon brush for all your cleaning. You may use an air compressor if it has a moisture trap on it, but you should remove the stitch plate and blow down and out through that opening. Your sewing machine mechanic will remove all the exterior covers before he blasts the machine with compressed air. You do not want to pack lint back into the machine.

A few tests you should know how to perform:

1. **timing:** To confirm that your machine is in the proper timing for the needle-and-hook relationship, insert a new needle, thread the machine, lower your tension a bit, and run your widest zigzag stitch. If the stitch forms on both sides, then your machine is well-timed.

2. **what's that ticking noise?** If you are concerned that you are hearing a ticking noise in your machine, remove the bobbin and bobbin case and the thread. Insert a new needle and run the machine with the presser foot in a position so that the feed dogs are not hitting the bottom of the presser foot (that would make a terrible noise) and listen for the tick. If no tick, then try it in your widest

zigzag; if still no tick, then thread the machine and replace the bobbin and bobbin case. If the tick returns, you know that it is simply the sound of the thread coming off of the position finger and that you do not need to be concerned.

3. **thread tension:** The most common mistake made in troubleshooting your thread tension is when you find big loops of thread on the underside of the fabric. Everyone blames the bobbin at first, but it rarely is the fault of the bobbin at all (Fig. 60). Big loops, ½ to 1 inch long, most often are caused by the thread not being in the upper tension correctly. Here is the key: The lifting of the presser foot opens the tension assembly on most home sewing machines. In other words, you must thread the machine with the presser foot in the highest resting position. The tension disks will be wide open to

Fig. 60

accept your thread. People often leave the foot down to prevent the fabric from slipping out of place as they rethread the machine. The needle must be up to thread, so we put the foot down. Oh, no. The thread will not be under tension, so it will make a bunch of noise and a big mess under the fabric. Now you are frustrated, so you lift the foot, pull the fabric out to clear the jam, and the next time you stitch, the tension is perfect. Baffled? Perhaps the tugging in frustration allowed the thread to get where it needed to be, and now you are ready to sew.

little loops, like specks on the bottom of the fabric, simply mean you need to tighten the top tension or loosen the bobbin. For speckling on the top, just loosen the top tension. If you still are getting irregular speckling, change your needle and match your threads; nobody is perfect. Just remember that you will become very familiar with your sewing machine, and you can care for it on a regular basis. Do not forget to have a full-service call done every few years by a professional, and make sure you get a detailed list of the work performed by the technician who cared for your machine.

organization:
ways to store it all

organization: ways to store it all

Touch these scissors . . . and die!
—*Anonymous*

never walk barefoot in your sewing area, especially if the floor is carpeted. Stepping on a dropped pin or needle can be very painful.

. . . .

there are essential furnishings and equipment required for a sewing area. You don't need much: a table for sewing, a space for cutting, an ironing board, a chair, and a light source. If you have the room you can leave your sewing area set up all the time. It's important to keep all of your sewing supplies together in one place so they're easy to gather when needed.

. . . .

some of us have dedicated sewing/craft rooms; others share space with a guest room; some have a sewing closet and some just a drawer or shelf. The task is making the most of the space we have, and the secret to that is organization.

. . . .

when you are sewing your floor can get covered with snipped threads and trimmings, and then they can get tracked all over the house. Here's a solution: Cut a piece of masking tape, strapping tape, or wide clear tape 12 inches long. Make a loop joining it to itself with the sticky side out. Press the join-up under the edge of your sewing table. Whenever you snip a thread just touch it to the tape. Replace the loop when it is full of threads.

....

if space is at a premium, we're forced to edit our sewing paraphernalia. Honestly, it's really not necessary to have six pairs of scissors and a huge fabric stash. Limited space can make us more efficient, because when we buy a piece of fabric we're forced to make it up so we can buy more. Now what's more fun than that?

....

a kitchen island is just the right height for a cutting table. No more sore back. If you're designing a sewing room, go to your local kitchen center for ideas.

....

check your local newsstand for Interweave's magazine *Studios*. It is jam-packed with ideas for real studios for real people.

....

it looks very nice and colorful to store your fabric stash on open shelves. But it's a really bad idea, as you can end up with faded fold lines from the light.

. . . .

plastic storage containers are a very good storage solution. Clear containers are a good choice, as you easily can see the contents. If your containers are opaque, attach an index card with the contents. This will keep your fabrics fresh and odor-free.

. . . .

if you have washed or steamed the fabric prior to storing, make sure it is totally dry before closing up a plastic container.

. . . .

thread can be very dangerous to our cats and dogs. They're curious, and before you know it they may eat a length of thread or pins or needles. Don't leave your pets by themselves around your sewing spot. If you suspect your pet has swallowed something, rush him or her to your veterinarian right away.

. . . .

keep a sewing journal. You'll thank us later for this piece of advice. Use plastic protector sleeves in a three-ring binder. For each project, slip in a photocopy of the pattern, a fabric sample, and a photograph of the finished project. Include the care instructions and fiber content of the fabric, any changes you made to the pattern, and suggestions in case you sew the pattern again. Also be sure to include any home decor projects you undertake. This will end up being a lifelong record of your projects.

. . . .

package directions for tools, notions, and fusible interfacings you have bought can be kept in plastic sleeves in your sewing journal.

. . . .

your binder can also store your idea clippings and any sketches you've made of contemplated projects.

. . . .

instructions from classes you've taken or special techniques you've clipped from magazines also should be placed in your binder. If you're really prolific, one binder may not be enough. If you accumulate a lot of clippings, categorize them and separate the categories with divider pages.

. . . .

for each piece of fabric in your stash, note the yardage, fabric content, and care instructions, plus when and where it was purchased and what it cost (this bit of information is just for the fun of it), on an index card. Staple a 2- by 3-inch sample to the card. When you need matching thread, fasteners, or other notions, just take the card shopping with you and you won't have to guess what will work. These cards can be stored in a recipe box. (If you're like us, you'll have lots of cards.)

....

organize your patterns in storage boxes. With the wide range of boxes available today you'll be able to find just the right size. Divide the patterns by category and separate them with cardboard dividers. Cut these dividers from poster board to fit the storage container. This will make it easier to find a specific pattern.

....

bet you have patterns you've never sewn and never will. It's time to purge them from your storage. Sell them on eBay and make a few dollars (especially if they are vintage), and just think: You're making room to buy more patterns.

....

you probably have fabric that you know you'll never use and don't even like. Bundle it up and take it to your local Goodwill drop-off, senior center, or group that sews for charity. There are plenty of people who would love to have your orphans. Most would be happy to have scraps, too.

....

to keep trash in your sewing area under control, store a small lined trash basket beside you and drop in your thread clippings, notches, trimmings, and so forth as you go, instead of letting them land on the floor. Then just lift out the liner when it fills up and throw it away. If you keep a few spares under the liner, the task is even easier.

....

a magnet with a telescoping handle is great for those pins that always seem to find their way to the floor.

....

make sure to pick up bobbins and pins off your floor before you vacuum. They can cause serious damage to your vacuum cleaner if they get stuck in the mechanism. Threads wound around the beater bar are a nuisance to remove.

....

inspiration

inspiration

Love is the thread that binds us.
—*Anonymous*

you are never too experienced to take a class and never too inexperienced, either. Check out your local school system or community college adult-education programs for class schedules and availability.

. . . .

start your own sewing library. Begin with *Vogue/Butterick Step-by-Step Guide to Sewing Techniques* or the *Simplicity's Simply the Best Sewing Book*, or the new *Threads Sewing Guide*. Add specialty books such as *Couture Sewing Techniques* or *Fine Embellishment Techniques: Classic Details for Today's Clothing.* For help with fitting try *Threads Fitting for Every Figure*.

. . . .

browse your local bookstore and the library to find other books you might like to add. Go to Amazon.com to check out the hundreds of sewing books on the market. You'll be amazed. Put the ones you like on your wish list. What better gift to receive than a book you'll use for years?

short of shelf space? Buy e-books and digital downloads instead. Some magazines offer DVDs of a whole year's issues. Isn't the electronic world wonderful?

start a subscription to a sewing magazine such as *Threads* magazine, *Sew Simple*, and *Stitch*. There are many more available. Again, go to your local bookstore and browse through its collection to find the magazines that speak to you. Take a couple home, and then subscribe to your favorites. Some magazines even have electronic editions available.

go shopping! See what is being shown in your town's retail stores. Look in all price points and you'll most likely get an idea or two you can take home to your sewing. Examine the details. Those touches are the things that don't show up on a pattern envelope but make a design your own.

browse through the latest fashion magazines for the fashion trends. Watch *Project Runway* on television to see how the designers solve the challenges. This is all fodder for your sewing.

....

are you computer savvy? If not, it's way past time to learn. The entire sewing world is open to you on the Internet. Just type your subject into a search engine and you'll be overwhelmed by the information available.

....

sewing communities abound on the Internet, and you can interact with thousands of other sewers on Web sites such as www.sewdaily.com and www.allfreesewing.com. Get involved and learn a lot.

....

pattern companies and sewing machine manufacturers all have Web sites full of information, and many have regular newsletters you can sign up for. See Resources for more information.

....

if you don't have a fashion fabric shop nearby, do not despair. Shop-by-mail sources abound on the Internet. Britex Fabrics at www.britexfabrics.com and Sawyer Brook at www.sawyerbrook.com are two well-known sources. Vogue Fabrics at www.voguefabricsstore.com offers a subscription swatching service, as do others. Go to www.threadsmagazine.com and search "online fabric shopping: a list of resources" for a list of online fabric sources.

resources

resources

Where happiness lives and memories are sewn.
— *Anonymous*

PATTERN COMPANY WEB SITES

Burda Style
www.burdastyle.com

Butterick Patterns
www.butterick.com

Independent Pattern Company Alliance
www.patterncompanies.com

McCall's Pattern Company
www.mccall.com

Simplicity Creative Group
www.simplicity.com

Vogue Patterns
www.voguepatterns.com

SEWING MACHINE COMPANY WEB SITES

Baby Lock
www.babylock.com

Bernina
www.berninausa.com

Brother International
www.brother.com

Elna International
www.elna.com

Husqvarna Viking
www.husqvarnaviking.com

Janome
www.janome.com

Pfaff
www.pfaff.com

Singer
www.singer.com

SEWING MAGAZINES

Sew Beautiful
www.sewbeautifulmag.com

Sew News
www.sewnews.com

Sewing World
www.sewingworldmagazine.com

Stitch
www.sewdaily.com

Threads
www.threadsmagazine.com

SEWING WEB SITES (THERE ARE MANY MORE)

All Free Sewing
www.allfreesewing.com

Burda Style
www.burdastyle.com

Pattern Review
www.patternreview.com

Sew Daily
www.sewdaily.com

Sew, Mama, Sew!
www.sewmamasew.com

Sew Simple
www.sewsimple.com

365 Days of Sewing
www.365daysofsewing.com

SEWING BOOKS (A FEW OF OUR FAVORITES)

Conlon, Jane. *Fine Embellishment Techniques: Classic Details for Today's Clothing.* Newtown, CT: Taunton Press, 1999.

Maresh, Janice Saunders. *Sewing for Dummies.* 3rd ed. Indianapolis: Wiley, 2010.

Shaeffer, Claire B. *Couture Sewing Techniques.* Rev. and updated ed. Newtown, CT: Taunton Press, 2011

Simplicity's Simply the Best Sewing Book. New York: Simplicity Pattern Company, 2003.

Stewart, Martha. *Martha Stewart's Encyclopedia of Sewing and Fabric Crafts.* New York: Potter Craft, 2010.

Threads Magazine. *Threads Fitting for Every Figure.* Newtown, CT: Taunton Press, 2011.

———. *Threads Sewing Guide: A Complete Reference from America's Best-Loved Sewing Magazine.* Newtown, CT: Taunton Press, 2011.

Vogue/Butterick Step-by-Step Guide to Sewing Techniques. New York: Sixth and Spring, 2012.

resources

ONLINE FABRIC SHOPPING

Britex Fabrics
www.britexfabrics.com

G Street Fabrics
www.gstreetfabrics.com

Sawyer Brook
www.sawyerbrook.com

Vogue Fabrics
www.voguefabricsstore.com

NOTIONS BY MAIL

Clotilde
www.clotilde.com

Nancy's Notions
www.nancysnotions.com

TRIMS BY MAIL

Button Emporium
www.buttonemporium.com

COLLECT ALL TITLES IN
THE POCKET POSH® SERIES!